A PRACTICAL GUIDE TO

IMPLEMENTING SCIENTIFIC SYSTEMS IN ACCOUNTING

A PRACTICAL GUIDE TO IMPLEMENTING SCIENTIFIC SYSTEMS IN ACCOUNTING

Rajesh Kandoi

Worldwide Published by
Pendown Press

PENDOWN PRESS LLP

An ISO 9001 & ISO 14001 Certified Co.,

Regd. Office: 3767A, Kanhaiya Nagar,

Tri Nagar, Delhi-110035

Ph.: 8130886000, 9650072927

E-mail: info@pendownpress.com

Branch Office: 1A/2A, 20, Hari Sadan, Ansari Road,

Daryaganj, New Delhi-110002

Ph.: 011-45794768

Website: PendownPress.com

Edition: 2025

Price: ₹ 299

ISBN: 978-93-6338-157-5

Layout and Cover Designed by Pendown Graphics Team

Printed and Bound in India by Thomson Press India Ltd.

वर्णानामर्थसंघानां रसानां छन्दसामपि।
मंगलानां च कर्त्तारौ वन्दे वाणीविनायकौ॥

To every ambitious business owner
who dares to think beyond limits,

To those stuck in chaos but
still dreaming of clarity and scale,

To those who believe there has to be a better way,

You're the reason this book exists.

Contents

Preface

Reaching a solid turnover means the business has found its footing—but that's just the beginning. Once you reach this stage, the real challenge begins: how do you continue to double your growth year after year? You've made it this far with your current systems, but now you need to rethink how you move forward. The systems and people that helped you reach this point might not be enough to keep you growing at the same pace. Until now, your business may have relied heavily on trusted individuals: one person handling sales, another managing procurement, and someone else in charge of accounting. This person-centric approach works for a while, but to reach the next level, you need to make a shift.

To continue growing year after year, you need to move from relying on people to relying on systems. This is where the power of automation and robust processes comes in. A key part of this transformation is the accounting function. Accounting is the brain of the business. It provides the information needed for management to make important decisions. However, many businesses find that their accounting department becomes overwhelmed by compliance work, repetitive tasks, and delayed reports. As a result, the ability to make timely, accurate decisions becomes compromised.

This book is specifically for business owners who are ready to take their businesses to the next level. Even if you've already reached a handsome turnover, this book will help you tackle the challenges of continuing growth. By focusing on creating a system that works independently of individuals, you'll be able to streamline your processes, increase efficiency, and most importantly, scale your business. With the right approach, your accounting department can become a solid foundation for future growth.

⦸⦸⦸⦸

Acknowledgements

Whatever I have achieved in life would have been impossible without the support of my parents, Sh. Ram Ratan Kandoi and Smt. Raj Kumari Kandoi. They have taught me unconditional love, and I have seen them grow along with me. The wings I have today would not have been possible without them.

To my wife, Sushmita, who has stood by me in every situation—you have handled all family responsibilities as well as business affairs with great skill and dedication. Thank you from the bottom of my heart.

To my children, Keshav and Raghav, who are the source of my happiness and inspiration—lots of love!

I am deeply grateful to my Guruji, my mentor, and my life guide, CA (Dr.) R. A. Kila ji, a true diamond connoisseur, who picked me as a rough stone and shaped me into a person people love.

My heartfelt gratitude to Rahul Jain and Akshar Yadav, who have shown me light and direction in times of confusion.

To our clients, who have shared their experiences and knowledge with us during this journey. Thank you for trusting us and being our inspiration.

A special acknowledgement goes to Dinesh Verma and his exceptional team at Pendown Press. From the initial concept to the final manuscript, their support and expertise have made this book possible.

And finally, to all my loved ones who have been with me on this journey—thank you for your unwavering support, encouragement, and affection. Even if your names are not mentioned, you always hold a special place in my heart.

Without the support of all of you, it would not have been possible for me to move forward with confidence.

Author's Corner

Many fast-growing businesses hit a stage where they feel stuck not because of lack of effort, but because their internal systems can't keep up with the pace. MIS reports are delayed or inaccurate, accounting feels chaotic, and key decisions are often based on guesswork rather than real-time data.

What these businesses now need is a robust, system-centric solution. They need a system that works smoothly no matter who is in charge. This is where I come in. I specialize in automating and streamlining the accounting and finance processes, ensuring that they are error-free, efficient, and independent of individual employees.

In many growing businesses, the accounting department is overwhelmed with repetitive tasks and government compliance work. As a result, they're unable to provide timely and accurate reports to the management. The reports that do come through are often delayed, and by the time they are reviewed, they lack relevance.

I help businesses develop systems where data input, processing, and output are handled seamlessly. I ensure that reports are generated in real-time, accurately, and consistently, so business owners and managers can make informed decisions when needed. By introducing automation and defining clear processes, I enable businesses to reduce human error and focus on growth.

In short, I create systems that allow accounting departments to function smoothly, without relying on any one person, and deliver the right information at the right time, every time. This way, businesses can scale with confidence and without the common hurdles of outdated processes.

This Book is Meant For...

For MSME Business Owners with a Good Current Turnover, Aiming for the Next Level

As a growing business owner, you may feel ready to take the next leap toward **exponential growth,** yet something invisible seems to be holding you back. This guide reveals that a **robust accounting system** is the hidden key to unlocking that growth. We'll take you on a four-phase journey designed to address your unspoken challenges: First, we'll identify the **pain points** you may be silently struggling with. Next, we'll offer a **diagnosis** of their root causes. This will lead to a powerful **revelation** about the true purpose of accounting; not just as compliance, but as a strategic asset. Finally, we'll present a **solution** framework based on the Input–Process–Output (IPO) model to bring order to the chaos and accelerate your business growth.

Throughout, you'll find authoritative insights delivered with a tone of ultimate expertise - expect to feel as though your every secret challenge has been understood and addressed. Let's begin this journey to transform your accounting from a necessary burden into a powerhouse for decision-making and sustainable growth.

Phase 1

Pain: The Hidden Problems in Your Accounting and Decisions

Every ambitious business eventually reaches a point where growth plateaus or problems start to emerge in unexpected ways. Often, it's not immediately clear that **faulty accounting practices** lie at the root of these issues. In fact, many MSME owners don't fully realize the *hidden accounting and decision-making problems* quietly brewing beneath the surface. Let's pull back the curtain on some of these silent pains:

- **Chaotic Financial Records:** Does closing the books feel like a fire-fight every month? Perhaps your team scrambles to reconcile numbers, finds transactions recorded incorrectly, or makes last-minute adjustments. You might dismiss it as part of the usual hustle of business, but it's actually a red flag. Businesses that lack **reliable accounting processes** often suffer "missed income and needless losses," with value slipping through the cracks unnoticed. In extreme cases, failing to maintain proper accounting can even mean underestimating earnings and drifting toward failure. The chaos in your books isn't just paperwork – it directly undermines your business's financial health and long-term stability.

- **Constant Cash Flow Crunches:** Many MSMEs experience a *rollercoaster* of cash - crazy ups and downs that feel hard to control. Do you often find yourself suddenly short on cash, rushing to pay salaries or clear vendor payments even when your sales are good? This usually means there's poor visibility (or simply, *you can't clearly see*) where your money is going. It's a classic sign of weak accounting. In fact, **78% of small businesses** report cash flow as a major challenge, and a staggering **82% of businesses fail due to poor cash flow management**. If cash is the lifeblood of your business, then bad accounting is like clogged arteries; it slows everything down. Without a clear, up-to-date system to track your incoming and outgoing money (*like who owes you, what you owe, and what's coming next*), you're basically running blind until a crisis hits.

- **No Clear View of Performance:** It's hard to make good decisions when everything feels foggy or unclear. Perhaps you realize you don't truly know which products or projects are profitable, which customers are driving costs, or why margins fluctuate. Without accurate, timely reports, you're left to *guess* which parts of your business are doing well and which aren't. Effective bookkeeping should give you "the clearest possible picture" of performance and areas to improve. If you're operating without that clear picture, you may be making decisions on false assumptions. Consider that inaccurate financial data inevitably leads to misguided choices - overestimating profits or misjudging expenses - resulting in overspending or missed opportunities. In short, unreliable numbers = unreliable decisions.

- **Surprise Compliance Issues and Penalties:** One of the most painful wake-up calls for a business is discovering a regulatory or tax issue they weren't prepared for. Do GST returns, tax filings, or audits turn into stressful ordeals at your company?
- Every year, thousands of promising Indian businesses collapse due to actions by tax authorities. The tragic truth? Over 68% aren't willful evaders — they're victims of 'small mistakes' in their accounts.
- If your accounting system isn't keeping you compliant by default, you end up in constant *reactive mode* - rushing to file returns, paying late fees, or fearing the next audit. Beyond the stress, the cost of non-compliance (penalties, fines, and legal trouble) can be steep and directly hit your bottom line. Hidden mistakes (an overlooked invoice here, a misclassified expense there) can snowball into legal troubles. The pain here is both financial and psychological - a constant, nagging worry that a compliance time-bomb might be ticking in the background.
- **Exposure to Fraud and Errors:** When your accounting process is weak or unorganized, it's not just about late reports; it also makes your business **vulnerable** to risks. Without proper controls, you might not notice if someone is misusing funds or if certain expenses are full of errors. Often, in many MSMEs, there's high trust within the team - *"we're all like family here"* - until one day, a betrayal or mistake is discovered too late.

A study by the Association of Certified Fraud Examiners found that businesses without simple internal controls (like routine checks or proactive data monitoring) experienced fraud **twice as often** as those with regular financial oversight. Weak accounting systems can become an open door for fraud or costly mistakes. The pain of such incidents is profound – financial loss, reputational damage, and the sting of realizing it could have been prevented with better systems.

These pains might feel uncomfortably familiar. Perhaps you've had an uneasy feeling about your finances, or a colleague hinted that your reports can't be fully trusted. The **ultimate pain** of all is that constant doubt – *"Can I really rely on my numbers?"* – a question that quietly shakes your confidence when it's time to make important decisions. But here's the good news: Recognizing these hidden problems is the first step. It sets the stage for our next phase, where we move from surface-level symptoms to root causes.

Phase 2

Diagnosis: Identifying the Root Causes of Accounting Chaos

So, why do these problems exist?

After all, you likely have an accountant or a finance team in place, and you *are* spending time and money on accounting. Why, then, does the chaos persist?

In this phase, we **diagnose the root causes** - the underlying issues in your accounting system that silently breed the pains we just explored. It's like a doctor examining the symptoms and saying, "Here's what's really going on." For most MSMEs facing these problems, the diagnosis boils down to four fundamental weaknesses:

- **Compliance Overload (Reactive Finance Function):** Too often, the accounting department is trapped in a never-ending loop of compliance tasks - GST filings, TDS, statutory audits, endless paperwork to satisfy regulators. These are important, but if **all** your finance energy goes into *feeding the compliance monster*, nothing is left for improving systems or providing strategic insights. Your team ends up **reactive**, always chasing deadlines, with no time to step back, plan, or analyze. This overload leads to burnout, more mistakes, and a narrow focus on just "getting things done.". It also conditions the business owner (you) to view accounting as a cost center that just "files return and keeps us out of jail." In reality, compliance should be the baseline, not the pinnacle, of your accounting function. When compliance work overloads your team, it's a sign the process isn't streamlined - maybe you're missing tools or training, or you haven't delegated routine tasks to software.

- **Key insight:** A finance team stuck in compliance mode cannot **support growth** or give you the clarity needed to make strategic decisions.
- **Lack of Standard Operating Procedures (No SOPs):** Does your accounting process rely on the heroics of individuals rather than standardized processes? For example, if one key accountant is on leave, does everything grind to a halt because *only they* know how to do certain tasks? This is what happens when **no documented SOPs** exist. Many small and mid-size companies overlook creating SOPs, thinking it's too "corporate" or unnecessary. But the truth is—having SOPs brings big benefits in consistency, speed, and control.

Without SOPs,

- The same task might be done differently by different people.
- Bank reconciliations are done well one month and skipped the next.
- Invoices might be filed in one folder today and a different one next week.

Such variability means errors slip through and accountability is blurred. SOPs are essentially **agreed-upon best practices** for your accounting workflows. When everyone follows them, work is consistent, and new staff can be onboarded quickly. If you lack SOPs, you lack control. And when things go wrong (as they inevitably do in business), you don't have a playbook to respond, leading to panic and last-minute fixes.

In short: no SOPs = no system, just individuals improvising daily. That's a root cause of chaos.

- **No Automation or Integration (Stuck in Manual Gear):** Are your accounting processes still heavily manual? Perhaps data from sales is manually entered into Tally or Excel by someone, or you maintain separate spreadsheets for inventory and then reconcile with accounting once a month. This lack of **automation** is a silent killer of both productivity and accuracy. Half of businesses today have started automating accounting tasks for efficiency, yet the other half remain stuck doing things by hand. If you're in the latter category, you're effectively *volunteering for repetitive work* and human error. Manual data entry, duplication of work across systems, and calculations done by hand - all these consume valuable time and introduce mistakes. They also keep your finance team bogged down in low-value tasks, instead of spending time on insights that could actually drive your business forward.
- Automation doesn't necessarily mean a fancy ERP implementation (though that can help) - it can be as simple as using better software, connecting systems via APIs or even using macros/scripts to eliminate repetition. The goal is to let machines do what they do best (repetitive calculations, data transfer) so humans can do what they do best (analyze, investigate exceptions, plan).

Without automation, your accounting process is slow, costly, and prone to mistakes. Transactions might not be recorded in real-time, leading to that *information lag* where you only find out something was wrong weeks later. In today's world, continuing without automation is like riding a bullock cart on a highway - it just isn't going to keep up.

- **Unreliable or Untimely Reports (Garbage In, Garbage Out):** If the inputs and process of your accounting are weak, it's no surprise that the outputs - your financial reports - will be **unreliable**. But this problem deserves special attention because it often becomes a vicious cycle. When the P&L or balance sheet you receive is full of errors, or the numbers just don't add up, you as a decision-maker start losing trust in the data. You might delay decisions or go with your gut, since the "facts" aren't clear. The finance team, in turn, may stop rigorously preparing good reports because they feel nobody uses them anyway. This creates a dangerous feedback loop.

- *But why are the reports unreliable in the first place?* Most likely because of the earlier points: data isn't captured properly (garbage in), processes aren't consistent (so errors not caught), and the team is too busy with compliance to double-check or analyze outputs. The result: **inaccurate financial data** making its way to your desk. And inaccurate data is worse than no data – it actively **misleads**. It can cause you to chase growth in an unprofitable segment, or miss a brewing liquidity crisis until it's too late.
- As an example, if inventory purchases are recorded incorrectly, you may think a product line is highly profitable, when in reality, hidden costs are eating away the margins. Or if sales are recorded on cash basis in one report and accrual in another, you get confusing signals.
- Inaccurate information "can have a significant impact on a business's growth, leading to poor decision-making, inefficiencies, and even legal or regulatory consequences". This is a direct quote from an accounting expert, and it rings true – bad info leads to bad choices.
- **Key insight:** Unreliable reports are both a symptom and a cause. They are born from poor processes, but they further perpetuate poor decisions. Breaking this cycle is critical.

In diagnosing these root causes, you might have a moment of clarity (and perhaps a bit of discomfort): *Yes, this is exactly what's happening in my business.* It can be eye-opening to realize that the finance function - which you assumed was "under control" - is actually operating with such flaws. But don't be disheartened: now that the real problems are identified, you can fix them. Just as a doctor's diagnosis, however troubling, is the first step to treatment, understanding that your **accounting system itself** needs improvement is empowering. It means the chaos is not inevitable - it has specific causes, which we can address logically with practical steps.

⦸⦸⦸⦸

Phase 3

Revelation: Accounting is More Than Compliance (Data to Decisions)

Now comes the "Aha!" moment - a revelation that can truly transform your mindset. Up to now, you might have thought of accounting as *just* bookkeeping, a necessary evil to file taxes and satisfy legal requirements. That view is common but **limiting**. The big revelation is this: **Accounting is not about tax returns and compliance paperwork - it's about converting raw data into vital information for better decision-making.**

In other words, your accounting department should be your information hub, not just a compliance cost center. When you shift your perspective to this, everything changes. Let's unpack this revelation:

Accounting = Information Processing, Not Just Number Keeping. Think of your business as a machine: every day it generates **data** - sales figures, expenses, inventory movements, production costs, payroll, etc. This raw data by itself is noise; it's scattered and difficult to use.

The real job of accounting is to **turn that noise into a clear, useful signal**. It's meant to **process** all those transactions into organized, accurate, and timely reports that tell you what's really happening. If the raw data is crude oil, accounting refines it into petrol - fuel for informed decision-making.

When done right, this process gives you sharp insights from a sea of numbers:

- "Product A has 20% higher profit than Product B."
- "We're taking too long to collect payments – in 2 months, cash flow might get tight."
- "Our marketing spend is working – it's bringing a 5x return."

These are golden insights that drive strategic moves. **This is the real purpose of accounting** - to empower you with information.

As one expert wisely put it, "Management accounting improves the decision-making process as it communicates decision-relevant insight and analysis to every decision-maker."

In other words, good accounting bridges the gap between data and decisions, ensuring that every decision-maker (from you as the owner to your managers) has the insight they need to act wisely.

Most SMEs Underutilize Accounting (and Suffer for It). It might surprise you, but studies have found that many small and mid-sized businesses *don't* use their accounting information effectively - and this greatly affects their success. In fact, one of the major reasons why so many SMEs struggle or shut down is because they don't use basic management accounting techniques. Many businesses don't fail because their products are bad or because there's no market. They fail because the owners don't have clear financial visibility – they can't see what's really going on in the numbers.

Think about it: if you don't know your true costs, you might price wrongly and lose money on each sale. If you don't track cash flows, you can run out of cash despite being "profitable" on paper. If you don't analyze trends, you can't anticipate downturns or seize opportunities in time. Essentially, treating accounting as "just compliance" is like having a powerful engine and using it only to honk the horn - you're missing out on its actual horsepower.

The revelation here is somewhat humbling: **the bottleneck to your next stage of growth might not be the market or competition, it might be your own underinvestment in financial systems and analysis.** The good news? This is fully under your control to change.

From Bean-Counter to Strategic Partner. A robust accounting system transforms the role of finance in your company. Instead of accountants being seen as bean-counters who just tally things for the taxman, they become **strategic partners** in your growth journey. Once they're free from routine compliance work, your finance team (or even outsourced accountants/CFOs) can offer you real value – like management dashboards, profitability analysis, cost-saving insights, risk assessments, and more.

This shift allows you to have forward-looking discussions like:

"Can we afford to open a new branch next quarter? What does the trend say?"

...rather than only backward-looking ones like:

"How did we do last quarter?".

Remember, **compliance is the floor, not the ceiling** - by complying with laws you keep out of trouble, but by leveraging accounting information you actively drive your business toward success. It's like the difference between a car's brakes and engine: compliance (and basic bookkeeping) keeps you from crashing, but the *engine* of insights is what propels you forward at high speed. Both are needed - but you can't win a race by only focusing on not crashing.

Let's illustrate the point with a simple scenario. Imagine two companies, A and B, both are in the same industry, both with Rs 100 Cr turnover.

- **Company A** treats accounting as a routine task - books are maintained to the minimum standard, primarily for year-end filing and taxes.
- **Company B**, sees accounting as a decision-making tool - they get weekly flash reports, track key ratios, and have automated many processes.

Now, imagine a new opportunity comes up - a smaller competitor is up for sale.

- **Company B** can quickly pull up projections, assess its financial capacity, evaluate the target's profitability, and make an informed bid within days.
- **Company A**, on the other hand, doesn't have up-to-date numbers or analysis; it either walks away blindly or stumbles through a due diligence, possibly overpaying or missing risks.

This same story plays out again and again: whether it's deciding pricing strategy, entering a new market, or cutting costs, the company with better financial insight will *always* have the advantage. In fact, they generate a virtuous cycle - good decisions lead to growth, which yields more data, which their accounting turns into even more insights, leading to further good decisions (exponential growth). The competitor stuck with compliance-only accounting gets left behind, making decisions on gut feel and outdated info, often with painful consequences.

Information is Power (When It's the Right Information). The revelation isn't just "accounting = information," but more precisely **"accounting = *quality* information."** It's not enough to drown in reports; you need reliable, relevant, and timely information. A robust accounting system will filter out the noise and present the key indicators that matter for your business. It will also ensure information is timely - a report that comes 3 months late is of historical interest only, not much use for agile decision-making. The aim is to turn your accounting into a

competitive advantage: you know your numbers inside-out, so you can move faster and smarter than other in your market. In a sense, robust accounting gives you *control*. It replaces the anxiety of not knowing with the confidence of having a handle on your business. Decisions that once felt like leaps of faith start to feel like calculated, data-backed moves. You can plan for exponential growth because you have visibility into the road ahead.

This is a profound shift. Many business owners describe it as a weight off their shoulders when they finally trust their accounting system. Instead of lying awake worrying about what surprise tomorrow's numbers might bring, they have dashboards on their phone with live data, and a finance team that proactively flags issues and opportunities. **This is the kind of setup we want for you. When done right, accounting becomes your partner, not your pain point.** When you truly grasp that accounting is about enabling good decisions, you'll start to demand more from it – and that mindset shift is half the battle won.

Phase 4

Solution: The Input–Process–Output (IPO)Framework to Fix Your Accounting

By now, we've identified your core challenges, traced their root causes, and redefined the real role of accounting in your business. Now comes the most crucial phase: the *Solution*. How do you bring order to accounting chaos and unlock the exponential growth you've been aiming for?

The answer lies in applying a **scientific method**—not guesswork, not trial and error. I recommend using the **Input-Process-Output (IPO) model**, a proven framework borrowed from systems engineering and quality management. This scientific approach breaks the entire problem into three actionable components, giving you a structured blueprint to strengthen your accounting system and, ultimately, your business decisions.

A **scientific method** is one that has been tested, validated, and consistently delivers results. I am not talking about theories—I am talking about a methodology that has worked across the board. I have personally implemented this system in over **750 businesses**, and the outcome has been remarkably consistent: clarity, control, and upward momentum. No detours. Just one direction—**upward**.

In a world where most MSMEs rely on instinct and patchwork solutions, this **scientific method** brings discipline, predictability, and results. It's your shortcut to building a reliable accounting backbone that drives intelligent growth.

At a high level:

- **Input:** What information and data you feed into your accounting system.
- **Process:** How that data is handled, processed, and managed inside the system.
- **Output:** What comes out at the end – the reports, information, and insights you get.

Think of this as a clear and logical blueprint for upgrading your accounting department — and in turn, improving your entire organization's decision-making power.

Using the IPO model ensures you address **every stage of the accounting information lifecycle**. It pushes you to think clearly about where things might be going wrong: Are the inputs flawed or incomplete? Is the process weak? Or are the outputs not meeting your needs? By systematically fortifying each stage, you end up with a comprehensive solution. Let's break down each component and see how you can implement changes in a very practical, logical way:

The Output:
Meaningful Information and Insight Out

You might be thinking, "The framework is called the IPO (Input-Process-Output) model, so according to it, Input should come first. But here, how is Output coming first?" It's an understandable thought. Let me explain how.

Generally, in our field, we focus first on the input—what kind of information, data, etc., needs to be put into the accounting system. But I approach it a little differently.

How?

I believe the very first step is to decide on the **Output** we require. There are two types of outputs we typically need. One is the output required by the government or regulators in the form of various returns and statements. This output is defined by law. The second type of output is the information you need as a business owner or management from the accounting department to take quality decisions. You can design the required reports and formats. So, the very first step is to decide on the output.

Once the output is defined, then determine the **Inputs** required to generate that output. For example, if you need to know product-wise sales or profits, project-wise sales or profits, territory-wise sales or profits, or employee-wise sales or profits, you will need the input data accordingly. With the help of experienced and expert professionals, you can identify what inputs are needed. After that, you design the **Process System** where these inputs will be fed. The system will then process the data and information to generate the desired output.

Think of it like cooking different dishes—every dish requires different ingredients, so the inputs aren't the same for all of them. Similarly, in this system, the inputs depend on the output you need.

This is how you first decide the required output formats of MIS reports you may require, and based on that, determine the inputs. Then, it can be figured out how to process these inputs using different software and experts to deliver the desired output.

A robust accounting system doesn't just generate standard financial statements; it delivers **useful insights, tailored to your business's needs, in a timely fashion.** The ultimate test of your accounting system is here: do the reports and analyses coming out help you make better decisions, faster?

Solution for Output: Focus on producing outputs that are **accurate, relevant,** and **actionable**, and ensure they reach the right people at the right time.

- **Accurate and Credible Reports:** Accuracy is non-negotiable. By fixing inputs and processes, you've largely ensured accuracy. However, it's still important to have a final review step for outputs. This could be a brief analysis every month of "what changed and does it make sense?" For instance, if profits suddenly dropped, is it correctly explained by a specific event (like one-time expense or seasonal dip)? Encourage your finance team to add a **commentary** to the numbers - a short explanation of key movements. This practice not only validates the accuracy (they might catch something that looks off and double-check), it also makes the numbers far more intelligible to you and others. When your outputs are accurate, you build a reputation for financial integrity. Stakeholders (banks, investors, board members) will trust your reporting. This can open doors: banks lend more easily, investors show interest, because they see you have your act together. Remember, earlier we noted that without accurate financial statements you may struggle to secure financing; conversely, solid financial reporting can **unlock growth capital opportunities**. It's hard to overstate how empowering it is to know that any given report - whether it's the monthly P&L or a project cost report - is spot on. That confidence makes decision-making much easier.
- **Relevant Management Information (KPIs & Dashboards):** Traditional accounting outputs include the profit & loss statement, balance sheet, and cash flow statement. These are important, but often they are not enough for day-to-day

management. You should define **Key Performance Indicators (KPIs)** for your business and have your accounting system report on them. These could be financial ratios (gross margin % or current ratio), efficiency metrics (inventory turnover or debtor days), or even non-financial metrics that accounting can help quantify (like sales per employee). Create a **dashboard** that gives you a snapshot of these KPIs. Many accounting software today allow customizable dashboards or you can use business intelligence tools linked to your accounting data. The idea is to have a one-page view of the health of your business.

For example, a dashboard might show:

- Today's sales,
- Month-to-date sales vs target,
- Cash on hand,
- Top 5 overdue debtors,
- Inventory level vs optimum,
- Key expense category trends, etc.

Decide what numbers truly matter to you and make sure the output includes them. This makes accounting output *actionable*. It's not just a report you file away; it's something that encourages you to take action. For example, if debtor days are increasing, you know it's time to have a meeting with your collections team. If gross margin is slipping, you investigate pricing or cost of goods. In short, design outputs that speak to your **strategy and operations**, not just outputs that satisfy GAAP or the tax department.

- **Timely and Frequent Reporting:** The value of information decays with time. Getting your financial statements six months after period-end is virtually useless for decision-making. Aim to get key outputs **quickly**. Thanks to the improved inputs and processes, you should be able to close books fast. For many MSMEs, a monthly reporting cycle is sufficient. Larger ones might do mid-month flash reports as well. The key is consistency - if you commit to a timeline (say, financial reports by the 5th of each month), stick to it. Timely outputs mean you are always steering the business with up-to-date information, akin to driving a car with real-time GPS rather than an old roadmap. Additionally, don't shy away from *real-time monitoring* of certain metrics. For instance, if cash is critical, get a daily automated report of bank balances and major outflows. If sales are volatile, set up a system to see sales data daily or weekly.

- Technology makes this easier - cloud systems can be accessed 24/7 from anywhere. You, as the owner, can have financial data on your phone when you travel. This kind of real-time visibility was once the luxury of large enterprises; now MSMEs can have it too with the right tools (many of which are affordable). By making outputs timely, you essentially tighten the feedback loop. You can react to issues or trends immediately, which is vital for capitalizing on opportunities or mitigating risks early.
- **Insight and Analysis (Beyond Numbers):** Ensure that the output stage includes **analysis**, not just raw numbers. Encourage your finance team or advisor to highlight anomalies, trends, and suggestions. For example, a simple variance analysis - actual vs budget or vs last year - with reasons can be hugely insightful. If expenses rose 10% last month, why? If a particular product line's revenue is declining, is it seasonal or a competitor's move? Numbers alone won't tell the whole story; analysis will. Some businesses create a brief monthly finance report or "management discussion" that accompanies the numbers, interpreting them in plain English. This is extremely useful for decision-making and also for sharing with other leaders in your company who may

not be financially savvy. Remember, **accounting information system's job is to not only provide data but make it meaningful**. You might even consider scenario analysis and forecasts as part of output - e.g., a rolling 3-month cash flow forecast that's updated each month, so you always see the road ahead. The **Output** stage is not static; it should evolve as your business questions change. If tomorrow you decide to explore a new venture, your accounting outputs might need to incorporate new metrics to evaluate it. A robust system is flexible to add new reports or dimensions of analysis.

Why This Matters: The **Output** is the payoff. It's where you, as the business leader, get the intelligence to make smarter decisions. When you have high-quality outputs, you've effectively turned your accounting system into a **competitive weapon**. It's no longer just a ledger; it's your business's cockpit instruments. Imagine flying a plane: inputs are like the various sensors feeding data, process is the computer crunching it, and output is your instrument panel telling you altitude, speed, fuel, etc. Without a good instrument panel, a pilot flies blind and risks a crash. But with it, they can soar to great heights. Similarly, with robust accounting outputs, you can navigate your company towards exponential growth with confidence. You'll spot storms on the horizon (and change course or prepare) and identify sunny opportunities (and speed toward them). Moreover, these outputs enable **accountability** within your team. When each department can see their numbers and KPIs, they take ownership. Your sales head can no longer say "I didn't realize our collections were slow" because it's right there in the dashboard; your operations head can't ignore rising costs because the reports flag it. Everyone starts aligning to data-driven performance, which boosts overall organizational effectiveness.

Finally, great outputs also enhance transparency and trust externally. You can share key metrics with potential investors to show traction, or with lenders to show creditworthiness. It moves the conversation from vague promises ("we think we're doing well") to solid facts ("here's the trendline of our customer acquisition cost and lifetime value, and why it's improving"). That credibility can attract partnerships and deals that fuel further growth.

The Input: Clean, Complete, and Timely Data In

"Garbage in, garbage out." This old saying is especially true in accounting. If your inputs - the raw financial data - are inaccurate, incomplete, or delayed, even the fanciest accounting software or the brightest CFO cannot produce good results.

Solution for Input: The goal is to capture **clean (accurate)**, **complete (nothing missing)**, and **timely (on time)** data. This means every invoice, expense bill, bank transaction, payroll entry - everything - must be recorded correctly and promptly. Here are some simple and effective ways to improve your data input:

- **Streamline Data Capture:** Wherever possible, **automate the data entry** process. Use integrated billing systems, POS systems, or bank feeds into accounting software to avoid manual re-entry. For example, sync your sales software with your accounting system so that every sale is recorded in the ledger in real time. Many MSMEs are adopting cloud accounting tools that pull data from various sources automatically. If you're using Excel or outdated software that doesn't integrate, it's time to evaluate modern solutions. Remember that while you're reading this, a competitor is automating what you still do manually, a startup is solving your customers' pain points better, and China is eyeing your market share. The clock isn't ticking - it's screaming. Automation not only saves time but also improves accuracy by eliminating human errors in data transcription. And when your input data is solid, the rest of the accounting process becomes much smoother and more valuable.
- **Standardize Data Collection:** Create **checklists and SOPs** for data collection. For instance, every expense claim by an employee must have a scanned receipt and proper approval before it's recorded. Every sales invoice must have a customer ID, date, amount, GST breakdown, etc., entered in a consistent and clear format. Train your team (and yourself) to follow these practices with discipline. Even small errors at the input stage (like a typo in the amount, or choosing the wrong account code) can snowball into major reporting inaccuracies later. It might feel boring or repetitive to be so strict about data entry, but the benefits are huge. Think of it like laying a strong foundation for a building - it's not glamorous, but everything stands sturdy because of it.

- **Real-Time or Daily Updates:** Move towards a model where financial data isn't updated just at month-end, but daily or in real-time. Today's tools allow for bank transactions to feed in daily, and sales/expenses to update continuously. When you have fresh data, you can make decisions on the fly. It also means that any errors are caught quickly. If a large expense was mis-classified today, your accountant can spot and fix it tomorrow, not 8 weeks later during quarterly closing. **Timeliness** of input is key. Many MSMEs suffer from "stale books" – where accounting only happens before audits or tax filings. That won't cut it for exponential growth. You need a live pulse on your finances.
- **Validity Checks at Entry:** Build in some basic validation at the point of entry. This can be as simple as setting up your software to alert if a duplicate invoice number is entered, or if an entry's debit and credit don't match, or if an unusually large transaction is being posted (perhaps flag it for review). Many accounting systems have these features; use them. The idea is to **catch garbage at the gate**. As an analogy, factories use quality checks for incoming raw materials - do the same for your financial data. As one source emphasized, if there's any "garbage in", the system will faithfully take that and produce "garbage out" reports. So, stop the garbage from entering in the first place.

Why this matters: By fixing the **Input** stage, you build trust in your data. When you look at numbers in your system, you know they're based on solid, verified entries. It sets a strong foundation. You cannot expect to get insightful outputs if the input data is flawed or incomplete - that would be like expecting a chef to make a gourmet meal out of rotten ingredients. Secure quality inputs, and you're already halfway to a robust system.

The Process:

Streamlined and Controlled Processing Inside

With clean data coming in, the next critical link is the **Process** - all the procedures and activities that happen to that data inside your accounting system. This includes recording transactions in the proper accounts, reconciling accounts, closing the books periodically, generating trial balances, and ensuring compliance tasks are done efficiently. A robust process is like the engine of a car: it takes fuel (data) and delivers performance (reports).

Solution for Process: Design your accounting processes to be **efficient, standardized, and well-controlled**.

Key actions to consider:

➢ **Document and Implement SOPs:** We return to SOPs because they are the backbone of any good system. Create a **Standard Operating Procedure manual for accounting** that covers all routine tasks -

- daily sales reconciliation,
- weekly bank reconciliation,
- monthly closing checklist,
- how to process vendor payment approvals

- payroll processing, etc.

This doesn't have to be hundreds of pages; even a concise document or flowchart for each major process is hugely helpful. Once these SOPs are in place, **train your team** to follow them rigorously. The difference will be night and day – tasks that used to depend on memory or individual skill become systematic. SOPs ensure every step in the accounting cycle is done the right way and at the right time, regardless of who is doing it. They "help standardize processes and ensure tasks are performed consistently," which reduces errors and variance. Consistency is *quality's best friend*. When your processes are standardized, you can start to rely on the output being consistently accurate.

- **Leverage Technology and Automation:** Just as in the input stage we want to automate data capture, in the **process stage we want to automate routine processing**. For example, if you can use software to auto-reconcile bank statements, do it – it will flag only the mismatches for human review, saving hours of effort. Use rule-based systems to auto-allocate common expenses to the right cost centers (many modern accounting software allow you to set rules, e.g., any transaction with description "Fuel" goes to Travel Expense). Implement an ERP or integrated accounting system if your scale demands it – something that links inventory, sales, and accounting in one. It brings everything into one place and removes the need for *manual juggling* across multiple software or spreadsheets.
- Remember the earlier stat: **robust accounting software allows you to handle more transactions without hiring more people**. This is crucial for growth – if your business doubles in size but your finance workload quadruples because you're doing things manually, that's not sustainable. A well-automated process scales gracefully. Today, there are even more powerful tools available:

- **Cloud accounting systems** that sync across devices
- **AI-powered invoice readers** that auto-fill fields
- **Dashboards** that update in real time

➢ The less time your team spends on data crunching, the more time they can spend on analysis (which is where you want them).

➢ **Internal Controls and Checks:** A robust process has checks and balances to maintain integrity. Introduce **internal controls** such as separation of duties (e.g., the person who approves payments isn't the one who cuts the cheque), approval workflows for expenses, and random spot checks. Even if you're a small or medium business, these simple controls can greatly reduce the chances of mistakes or fraud. For instance, if two different people independently reconcile a key account and the results differ, that triggers an investigation that can catch a mistake early. Also, ensure that your accounting software keeps **audit trails** (logs that show who made changes and when). That 'undo' button you've been relying on? It's now a digital trail. In the era of forensic auditing, every backdated or altered voucher waves a red flag at tax authorities—and auditors treat corrections like crime scene evidence.

➢ **Regularly Back Up Your Data Offsite** (like using cloud storage). A lost or corrupted file with no backup can set you back months, which is an avoidable disaster. Additionally, consider having an *external advisor or auditor* periodically review your processes - not just the financials, but the **process**. They can often spot weaknesses you overlooked. Think of it as a health check for your accounting engine.

➢ **Regular Closing and Reporting Cycles:** Make sure you have a regular rhythm to your accounting process. For example,

monthly closing of accounts by the 5th of the next month, and a management review by the 7th. This way, you're always in touch with your numbers. It also prevents the last-minute quarter-end or year-end panic because you've been keeping up along the way. A well-oiled process will churn out financial statements periodically like clockwork. Many MSMEs suffer from what I call "FYI Syndrome" - *Fix Yearly, Ignore in-between*. They only fix the books when the annual audit is due. That won't work if you want to join the big leagues of growth. You need "close and repair" happening continuously. By instituting monthly (or even weekly for some metrics) closes, you force the process to reveal and correct any issues ongoingly. Over time, you'll notice the closes get smoother, faster, and less fraught with adjustments - a sure sign your process maturity is increasing.

Why this matters: The **Process** stage is where your accounting system either adds value or creates bottlenecks. A streamlined process means lower costs (less wasted time, fewer errors to fix) and faster reporting (you get info when it's still relevant). It also means your finance team can handle more transactions and complexity without cracking. This is vital for scaling up. If doubling sales means double the accounting work, you'll feel reluctant to grow further because the back-office can't keep up. The right processes, supported by technology, can often handle exponential growth in volume with little or no increase in effort.

Professionally managed processes also inspire confidence beyond your four walls - investors, banks, or partners can see when a company's finance operations are tight. It reflects good governance. By focusing on process, you are essentially **building an accounting machine that runs smoothly in the background**, letting you focus on the business. Think of companies that went from startups to IPOs - one thing they all have in common is they invested in solid financial systems early. They had to, because nobody will invest or buy a company with messy books. By adopting that mindset now, you're future-proofing your business. Remember, robust processes **prevent small problems from snowballing**. They give you early warning of issues and the flexibility to address them before they become painful, and they also ensure opportunities (like suddenly available cash to invest) are visible to you. In essence, you move from firefighting to **fire prevention** and optimization.

Bringing It All Together: The IPO Model in Action

By addressing **Input, Process, and Output** in a structured way, you create a self-reinforcing system. High-quality inputs feed efficient processes, which produce reliable outputs, which in turn validate and encourage even better inputs (because when your team sees their work translating into meaningful results, they're motivated to maintain quality). You're no longer just crunching the numbers—you're building a **living, breathing accounting ecosystem** that continuously turns data into insight, chaos into order, and uncertainty into confident action.

It's worth noting that this Input-Process-Output framework isn't a one-time setup. It's an *iterative cycle*. You don't fix it once and forget it. You will continuously monitor each stage:

- **Are we capturing all inputs as the business expands?** (e.g., if you add a new sales channel, is its data integrated?)
- **Are our processes scaling and adapting?** (e.g., as transaction volumes grow, do we need to automate more or add an extra check here or there?)
- **Are our outputs still aligned with our goals?** (e.g., if you launch a new product line, you might need new reports to track it).

Think of IPO as a cycle of ongoing improvement. Many leading companies adopt this mindset - continuous improvement of their systems - which keeps them agile and ahead of the curve. As you grow, new challenges will come, but with an IPO framework, you'll tackle them methodically: identify if it's an input issue, process issue, or output requirement, and address accordingly.

Importantly, implementing the IPO solution doesn't necessarily mean doing it all alone. You might engage consultants to help set up systems, invest in training your staff, or outsource parts of the process if needed (for example, outsourced bookkeeping or CFO services can temporarily fill gaps until your in-house capabilities are strong). The key is that **you, as the business leader, understand this framework and drive its adoption**.

Finally, don't overlook culture: your team needs to understand why these changes are happening. Share with them the vision - that by building a better accounting system, the company will grow faster and everyone benefits. Often, finance teams in MSMEs are yearning to do more insightful work but are stuck in the rut of how things have always been done. Empower them with this model and watch them transform from bean-counters to business partners.

Let's recall our journey briefly: we started with *pain*, the troubling symptoms many businesses face; we found the *diagnosis*, the underlying causes; we experienced a *revelation* that pointed us in a new direction; and now we've outlined the *solution*, the concrete steps to take. This psychological and logical progression is intentional - because meaningful change in a business happens not just with systems and processes, but with mindset. By following through these phases, you're not only installing a new accounting framework, you're instilling a new culture in your company: one that values accuracy, efficiency, and insight in financial management. One that encourages your team to move from reactive number-tracking to proactive decision-making. The payoff of this will be seen in your bottom line and in your ability to execute ambitious strategies. Teams work better, leaders decide faster, and growth becomes not just possible but predictable.

To reinforce why this solution matters: A review of multiple studies has proven that adopting strong accounting information systems and practices **directly improves SME performance, decision-making, internal controls, and transparency**. In essence, what we're proposing is not theoretical - it's backed by research and the experience of numerous successful businesses. Robust accounting is the foundation on which sustainable, exponential growth is built. Companies that get this right are the ones that break out of the SME bracket and become industry leaders. You've already achieved a lot to reach here; the next leap will demand an even greater level of management finesse. And that's exactly what the IPO accounting framework empowers you to achieve.

Conclusion: Take Charge of Your Accounting Future

You've now seen the full picture of why a robust accounting system is **essential** for your next stage of growth. No more treating accounting as a back-office afterthought or a mere compliance requirement. It's time to approach it as a *strategic function* that can drive decisions, reveal opportunities, and safeguard your business's health. The pains we discussed - the confusion, the uncertainty, the constant firefighting - **do not have to be "just part of doing business."** They are problems you can solve. And by solving them, you unlock a new level of freedom.

- Freedom from **guesswork**.
- Freedom from **crisis-mode.**
- Freedom to **lead with clarity and control**.

Imagine this: You walk into your office knowing exactly where your business stands. Real-time numbers at your fingertips. Trends clearly visible. A forward-looking plan built on **solid, trustworthy data**. That's not a dream; that's the reality a well-implemented IPO framework can deliver. And the **peace of mind** that comes with it? Truly priceless.

Adopting the Input-Process-Output framework will require some effort and possibly changes to long-established habits. But remember, you're not doing this for the sake of accounting itself

- you're doing it to enable **exponential growth**, to outmaneuver competitors, to seize market opportunities before they do, and to sleep better at night knowing your company's financial brain is switched on and working for you.

You're creating an **engine for growth**. As you implement these changes, even gradually, you'll start noticing improvements: fewer errors, faster closes, more insightful conversations in management meetings, and yes, likely improvements in profitability and cash flow as leaks are plugged and insights acted upon.

That's the ripple effect of robust accounting. It starts behind the scenes... but ends up transforming every department, every decision, and every outcome.

To help you move forward on this journey, here are a few **actionable next steps** you can consider (no strings attached, purely for your benefit):

➢ **Self-Assessment Checklist:** Clarity begins with honesty. I've created a **free self-assessment checklist** to help you take a clear-eyed view of where your accounting function stands today. This simple yet powerful tool lets you evaluate key areas like:

- Timeliness of reporting
- Frequency of errors
- Level of process documentation
- And more

Many business owners **feel** something isn't right but can't always pinpoint the exact issue. This checklist brings hidden gaps to light in **black and white**. Use it with your finance team; it can spark productive discussions and help prioritize what to fix first. Small clarity steps often lead to big transformation.

- **Ready-to-Implement SOP Templates:** Writing SOPs from scratch might feel daunting. To make it easier, you can access a set of *sample Accounting SOP templates* (also provided free as part of this guide's resources). These cover common processes like Accounts Payable, Accounts Receivable, Month-End Close, Expense Approval, etc. You can customize them to your business. Even if you have some SOPs, comparing them with industry best-practice templates could show you if something important is missing. Adopting standard templates can jump-start your documentation effort and ensure you're covering all bases.
- **A Key Point to Add:** Another crucial aspect to consider is creating a system for regularly updating SOPs and training your staff. Often, businesses create SOPs just for the sake of it, but they aren't followed up consistently. Whether there are changes in business requirements, frameworks, or regulatory updates, the biggest impact is on the SOPs. Without timely updates, they become isolated and irrelevant, eventually becoming "dead" documents that no one uses.
- To prevent this, it's essential to focus on evolving your SOPs and creating a robust training system for your staff. This ensures that no matter who joins or leaves your team, the process continues seamlessly, and everyone is aligned with the latest procedures and standards. SOPs shouldn't be static—they should evolve with your business.
- **Risk & Efficiency Calculator:** Sometimes, quantifying the impact of poor accounting systems can build the case for change (especially if you need to convince partners or invest budget). I offer a *Risk & Efficiency Calculator* tool where you input a few facts about your current processes (e.g., number of manual entries, frequency of errors noticed, days to close books, etc.), and it will estimate the potential cost of those

inefficiencies and risks to your business. It will also project the savings or benefits if you improve those metrics (for instance, how much more cash you'd have if debtor days are reduced by 10% due to better tracking). Seeing the rupee value of inefficiency often drives home why this initiative is worthwhile. Plus, you can use this to prioritize - address the highest value gaps first.

Feel free to use these tools in whatever way suits your pace and priorities - they are there to support your journey. Implementing change is always easier with the right resources and benchmarks in hand. Importantly, these tools are *educational*. They'll likely trigger new questions and insights as you fill them out, further enhancing your understanding of your business's financial dynamics.

A Journey That Compounds Over Time: In closing, remember that **robust accounting is a journey, not a one-time project**. But it's a journey that pays dividends at every step. Every improvement you make - whether it's catching errors earlier, speeding up reporting by a day, or getting a clearer KPI - immediately contributes to better decisions and smoother growth. Over time, these improvements compound. What you want is to reach a tipping point where your accounting system becomes self-sustaining and continuously improving. At that stage, you as the business owner, can truly step back from micromanaging finances, confident that the machine is running well, and devote your energy to strategy, innovation, and expansion. These are the areas that multiply your business 10x. That's the real promise of fixing your accounting: **it frees you to focus on exponential growth**, with the assurance that the financial foundation is solid, stable, and supporting you.

Your business has tremendous potential. By fortifying your accounting function, you're effectively building a launchpad for that potential. So take that step – have the tough conversations, invest in the right tools, get the right advice, and implement the IPO framework. The road to exponential growth is wide open for you, and now you have the map to navigate it with precision. Here's to your success and to a future where your accounting system is no longer a source of headaches, but a source of strength and competitive advantage.

⊘⊘⊘⊘

DIY or Do It with Me

Option 1: The Independent Path - "Make It Happen"

You've just armed yourself with the battle-tested strategies that have transformed 750+ businesses into financially invincible forces. But knowledge without action is like an unloaded weapon - it makes noise but wins no wars.

Embrace these changes. Utilize the free checklist, SOP templates, and risk calculator shared with you, and witness firsthand how a reimagined accounting system can power your MSME's next leap. This is your time to take full control of your finances and future.

As my heartful thank you for walking this journey with me, I'm gifting you what my Rs 50,000/day clients receive - your AI-Powered Customized Accounting Manual:

1. Instant Rulebook: Drafted by our expert team + AI to your business specifics
2. Checklists That Prevent 92% of Errors
3. Free Lifetime Updates as laws evolve

Scan the QR Code Now → Answer quick questions → Get your gift in 72 hours**

No upsells. No conditions. Just one warrior's gift to another.

Because Bharat's economic dawn needs you battle-ready by sunrise. When you're ready, you can also reach out for a complimentary consultation purely as a fellow professional who wants to see you win.

You've got the tools. Now make it happen.

Option 2: The Partnership Path – "Let's Build It Together"

If you prefer to walk this path with someone experienced by your side, I'm here to support you. Whether you need help refining your SOPs, improving reporting, or navigating the IPO framework, I can guide you step by step with solutions tailored to your stage of growth.

This is not about a sales conversation. It is a professional collaboration driven by a shared belief in your business potential.

You are not just ready for growth. You are built for it. Let's put the right financial systems in place and unlock the scale, control, and clarity your business truly deserves.

You can schedule a one-to-one meeting with me for personalized guidance. Just drop a message or write to me at **ask@rajeshkandoi.com** to get started.

Let's make your accounting system your greatest strategic advantage. Together.